Reel It In

ICE FISHING

Tina P. Schwartz

PowerKiDS press™

New York

To Bauer Gucky… an honorary Schwartz kid. With love, Mrs. Schwartz.

Published in 2012 by The Rosen Publishing Group, Inc.
29 East 21st Street, New York, NY 10010

First Edition

Editor: Amelie von Zumbusch
Book Design: Kate Laczynski

Photo Credits: Cover, pp. 5, 6, 7, 9 (bottom), 12, 13 Shutterstock.com; p. 4 © www.iStockphoto.com/Michael Olson; p. 8 © www.iStockphoto.com/Vladimir Gurov; p. 9 (top) Greg Ceo/Getty Images; pp. 10–11 Hemera Technologies/AbelStock.com/Thinkstock; p. 14 © www.iStockphoto.com/Jennifer Daley; p. 15 © Nordic Photos/SuperStock; pp. 16–17 © www.iStockphoto.com/Marcel Pelletier; p. 18 iStockphoto/Thinkstock; p. 19 Photos.com/Thinkstock; p. 20 Wayne R. Bilenduke/Getty Images; p. 21 Elsa/Staff/Getty Images Sport/Getty Images; p. 22 © www.iStockphoto.com/Steve McSweeny.

Library of Congress Cataloging-in-Publication Data

Schwartz, Tina P., 1969–
  Ice fishing / by Tina P. Schwartz. — 1st ed.
      p. cm. — (Reel it in)
  Includes index.
  ISBN 978-1-4488-6200-9 (library binding) — ISBN 978-1-4488-6359-4 (pbk.) —
ISBN 978-1-4488-6360-0 (6-pack)
  1. Ice fishing—Juvenile literature. I. Title. II. Series.
  SH455.45.S39 2012
  688.7'69—dc23

                                    2011029906

Manufactured in the United States of America

CPSIA Compliance Information: Batch #WW12PK: For Further Information contact Rosen Publishing, New York, New York at 1-800-237-9932

CONTENTS

Ice Fishing Is Fun!

You might get cold while ice fishing, but you do not need to worry about mosquitoes and other bugs, as you would in the summer.

Have you ever wanted to go out onto a frozen lake or pond to catch fish? If so, you would love a sport called ice fishing! Ice fishing is a winter sport. It happens only in places where it gets so cold in the winter that lakes and other bodies of water become covered in ice. You have to make sure the ice is at least 4 inches (10 cm) thick to walk on it and ice fish safely.

You must dress warmly for ice fishing. You need special fishing gear, or **tackle**, too. There are even little houses you can fish in!

Ice fishing is a popular sport in places that have long, cold winters.

Where Do Fish Go in Winter?

Fish that live in cold parts of the world have different ways of surviving the winter. Some **hibernate**, or slow down their breathing to sleep all season. Bass, sunfish, and catfish do this. Their bodies cannot adjust to swimming

This man caught a northern pike while ice fishing. These fish are often just called pike.

Yellow perch, such as this one, are among the fish people often catch when they go ice fishing.

around in the freezing cold water. They move to the edge of a stream or pond and settle their bodies into some mud or leaves.

Other fish, such as trout, salmon, pike, and yellow perch, still swim around in the cold water under the ice. These fish often swim down to the deepest parts of lakes or rivers because the water is warmer there.

What to Bring

For ice fishing, you need to wear many layers of clothing to keep you warm. It is better to wear too many clothes than too few. You can remove a layer or two if you get too warm. You should wear boots so you do not slip. They should be very warm as well.

Remember to dress warmly when ice fishing, as this girl has done.

You will also want to have mittens or gloves, a scarf, and a warm hat. A jacket with **reflectors**, or glowing tape, is useful so that people on **snowmobiles** can see you if it gets dark. Waterproof and windproof gear is good so you do not get cold and wet while fishing.

Ice skates are one of several ways to get around on a frozen lake. People also walk carefully in boots. If there is thick snow on the ice, people may wear snowshoes.

9

When and Where to Ice Fish

These people are ice fishing on Lake Saint-Louis, near Montreal, Quebec. Ice fishing is common in Canada and in many northern US states.

10

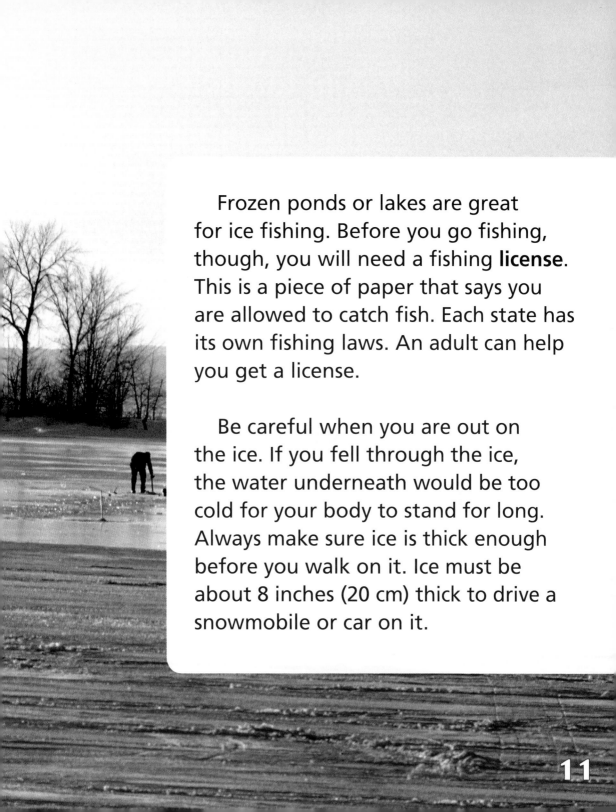

Frozen ponds or lakes are great for ice fishing. Before you go fishing, though, you will need a fishing **license**. This is a piece of paper that says you are allowed to catch fish. Each state has its own fishing laws. An adult can help you get a license.

Be careful when you are out on the ice. If you fell through the ice, the water underneath would be too cold for your body to stand for long. Always make sure ice is thick enough before you walk on it. Ice must be about 8 inches (20 cm) thick to drive a snowmobile or car on it.

Drilling the Hole

To ice fish, you will need to make a hole in the ice. This is often done with a kind of drill called an **ice auger**. The hole should not be more than 1 foot (30 cm) across. When ice is not as thick, you can make a hole with a tool

This boy is drilling a hole with an ice auger. Only use an ice auger if an adult is there to make sure you are using it right.

There are several kinds of ice augers. This ice fisherman is using a motor-driven one.

called an **ice chisel**. Ice chisels are also called spuds. They look like poles and are used to chop into the ice. Make sure to tie the ice chisel around your arm with some string. That way it will not fall to the bottom of the lake if it slips out of your hands!

Ice-Fishing Gear

You need a lot of fishing gear and safety gear to go ice fishing. It helps to have a sled to carry it all around on, such as the one this girl is pulling.

The rods used in ice fishing are much shorter than those used in summertime fishing. They are usually between 2 and 5 feet (61–152 cm) long.

Even more important than what rod and **reel** you choose are the safety items for ice fishing. A

life preserver will keep you safe if you fall in the water. If you have trouble, such as if you or someone you are with falls through ice, you should have a whistle to get attention. Carry a cell phone in a plastic bag, too. A **compass** can show you what direction you are facing so you do not get lost on a big lake.

If you fall through the ice, it is important to get out of the water as quickly as you can. Once you are out, you will need to dry off and warm up quickly, too.

Ice-Fishing Methods

There are three ways to ice fish. The first is with a rod and reel, as people do in the summertime. The second way is with tip-up flags. You set up your line in the water, with the flag pointing down. The flag will flip up when a fish bites your line.

This woman is checking on one of the tip-ups she set up. People often set up several tip-ups in a row and keep an eye on all of them.

The last method is with a spear. Ice-fishing spears have several sharp points. You may need to make a bigger hole in the ice if you are spear fishing. You must pay closer attention, too. You actually watch the water through the hole in the ice. When a fish comes into view, jab it with your spear.

FUN FISH FACT

When ice fishing, you can use the catch-and-release method. You carefully take the fish out of the water, remove the hook from its mouth, and release it back into the wild.

Shelters

Ice-fishing shelters that are made of wood or something else sturdy are often known as ice-fishing sheds, shacks, or cabins.

Some ice fishermen sit on stools in the open air to fish. Others use a **shelter** to keep out the cold weather. There are several kinds of shelters. Windbreaks block out the wind on two or three sides. Collapsible shelters fold up. They are light and easy to carry around. Mobile shelters can also be moved around and are a bit sturdier.

Portable shelters have hard floors and cloth coverings over metal frames. People usually put them up and take them down each time they fish. Permanent shelters look like tiny cabins. They are usually made out of wood. People leave them on the ice for the whole winter.

In some spots, people set up so many ice-fishing shelters that it looks like there is a village on the ice! These ice-fishing shelters are on the Sainte-Anne River, in Quebec.

Why People Ice Fish

In many countries, people once ice fished to find food to eat during the winter. Now ice fishing is done mostly for fun. Ice fishing is popular in parts of the American Midwest where the winters tend to be cold. In fact, ice fishing is so popular that winter fishing

The peoples of the Arctic have a long history of ice fishing. This Inuit man is using a harpoon to fish in Nunavut, Canada. Harpoons are spear-like tools that people use to hunt or fish.

makes up one-quarter of the yearly catch in the state of Wisconsin.

People like ice fishing for different reasons. Some people ice fish alone and enjoy that quiet time. Others fish in groups and enjoy spending time with friends and family. Still others like taking part in ice-fishing **competitions**.

These people are at an ice-fishing competition in Brainerd, Minnesota.

The Future of Ice Fishing

Today, people have special tools to help them find fish under the ice. One is **sonar**. Sonar gives off sound waves and picks them up again after they bounce off things underwater. It shows fishermen what is under the ice. They use sonar to learn how deep the water is. It shows them where weeds and fish are, too.

Ice fishing is fun. It also gives you an excuse to spend time on a beautiful, if chilly, frozen lake.

Underwater cameras also help people find fish while ice fishing. They can give fishermen clear pictures of what is under the ice. Ice fishing gets more advanced every day!

GLOSSARY

compass (KUM-pus) A tool made up of a freely turning magnetic needle that tells which direction is north.

competitions (kom-pih-TIH-shunz) Games.

hibernate (HY-bur-nayt) To spend the winter in a sleep-like state.

ice auger (YS AH-gur) A tool for making holes in ice by drilling into it.

ice chisel (YS CHIH-zul) A tool for making holes in ice by chopping away at it.

license (LY-suns) Official permission to do something.

life preserver (LYF prih-ZER-ver) Something that floats and is used to keep people safe during water activities.

reel (REEL) Something around which line or thread is wound.

reflectors (rih-FLEK-terz) Things that throw back light.

shelter (SHEL-ter) A place that guards someone from weather or danger.

snowmobiles (SNOH-moh-beelz) Vehicles made to travel over the snow.

sonar (SOH-nahr) A type of machine that helps people tell what kinds of things are underwater.

tackle (TA-kul) The gear and tools used for a hobby.

INDEX

WEB SITES

Due to the changing nature of Internet links, PowerKids Press has developed an online list of Web sites related to the subject of this book. This site is updated regularly. Please use this link to access the list:
www.powerkidslinks.com/reel/ice/